Advanced Search Engine

Advanced Search Engine Optimization

A Logical Approach

Terry Dunford II

American Creations of Maui
Wailuku, Maui, Hawaii

American Creations of Maui
45 Uahaa Pl., Wailuku, HI 96793

ISBN: 978-06152-0506-9

Special thanks to my wife, Debra, who has supported me in my work while I spent hours and hours and hours performing, researching, and writing about search engine optimization and internet marketing. Without her support, this publication would not have been possible.

Table of Contents

Introduction

Websites are unquestionably the most overlooked means of marketing for local, owner-operated businesses. It is a verifiable truth that every business owner **NEEDS** a website. In this article, I will explain why every business needs a website and how a business owner can go about obtaining one.

A website is the most important thing that you can invest in to guarantee that your business competes and thrives among the many competitors inhabiting your particular market. An online presence is the most efficient and economical way to reach more people who are seeking exactly what you provide. Furthermore, it will ensure that your business will accrue the profits it should. Possessing an online store, if you are selling products, is the smartest and easiest way to conduct business across the globe. Anyone can acquire a website and it is strikingly affordable compared to other marketing techniques like costly advertising, Yellow Page listings and the list goes on and on.

In today's market, running a small business of any kind has never been so competitive. Even specialty markets can have an abundance of competitors in the immediate vicinity. By having an online presence, you earn respect, create a sturdy foundation, enable enhanced communication, and reach a larger customer-base. The possibilities of success escalate once you have a website!!!

It is very likely that you have encountered your competitors online. You observe their nice website that reaches many more consumers than businesses who are lacking the one thing that we should never be without – **A WEBSITE**.

It is much easier to have someone visit your website, than to drive to your store to see what you have to offer. Everything they need to know can be conveniently located on your website and even a way to purchase the product (which is optional of course, but extremely recommended).

Now that you understand the importance of having an online presence, here are a few things that you should consider:

Constructing Your Website

A properly developed website permits your prospective consumers to gather the information they require from the solitude of their own home. There are a few questions that you should ask yourself when deciding on what content to include on your web site. For example, what questions are frequently asked about your product or service? And how, precisely, is the best way to explain that question on your website to clarify it to a potential consumer? This is the information that needs to be accessible on your new website. If you have a Frequently Asked Questions (FAQ) page, directions, how-to's, etc..., then customer phone calls will be minimal compared to not having an informative website. Let the website give customers' everything they need to know about your product, how to order, and all other information that may be relevant to your product or service.

Target Market

Visualize yourself as a customer and study all the

information on the site. Investigate all the content, its relevancy and importance. Furthermore, ensure that it is attractive enough to catch the attention of visitors who might have inadvertently entered your website. Your target market is any person willing to purchase your product or service. The website should have appropriate information and be regularly maintained for optimal performance.

Visual Aids

There should be visual aids on your site that visually explains your product or service. If you are an artist and are selling your artwork, then you should have photographs of your artwork so prospective buyers can observe what you have to offer. Endeavor to construct the site to be an eye-catching, fun and interesting site that will attract visitors' attention. A visually appealing website will be more successful than an amateur site because visitors will be more attracted and, consequently, become more interested in your product or service because you have caught their "eye".

Competing in Today's Market

To stay on top of an ever-growing market, most business owners try to keep tabs on their competitors and employ professional marketing specialists. By doing so, they ensure that their business will stay competitive and retain the customer-base. Search Engines generate about 95% of all visitors to websites. Your marketing focus should be directed towards optimizing your site with the search engines to increase your keyword rankings. As your keywords begin increase in rank, then you will notice that your traffic will begin to increase.

Benefits of Having an Online Store

Ebay isn't the only venture that thrives on the internet. Small business owners are finally discovering the power of the worldwide web. Do you have a product that can be shipped? If so, you are the perfect person to obtain an online store. A website can handle everything from attracting potential customers to your product, to accepting credit card payments directly from your website, and to answer all of your customer's questions about shipping times, prices and information about the product. Having a website can also reduce printing costs normally associated with store catalogs, brochures, postcards, and the countless other methods of advertising from the past.

A website promotes a professional image for any business. Customers anticipate businesses to already have a website and more customers are reaching for their mouse to explore a business service or product prior to purchasing. A website can even help a home business acquire and maintain a professional image.

Having an online presence by acquiring a website is a lucrative approach to promote your business. Websites do not cost a lot of money to develop and will definitely be worth the small investment. A small business owner could easily spend thousands a year just to be in the local Yellow Pages. Bearing in mind that you have the chance to reach millions of prospective consumers, getting a website is a profitable method of reaching your target market.

1

Reaching the Top

Search engine optimization **(SEO)** is the most vital responsibility a site owner can perform to ensure success. Over 92% of all traffic to websites is from a search engine. Therefore, to guarantee traffic you have to do what is essential so that your primary keywords escalate to the very top of the search engines. I will provide the knowledge necessary to engage a successful SEO journey. I will enlighten you to the top three factors in getting high rankings.

(Figure 1.1)

Undoubtedly, the most imperative onsite factor is to integrate your site's primary keyword in the Title Tag, as illustrated above in *figure 1.1*. The Title Tag is the very first html tag under the first starting tag. The Title Tag information appears on the very top left of the internet browser. Search engines also use the title tag information for the outgoing links to websites. Additionally, there are several basic guidelines that must be followed when writing the content of the Title Tag. First, it's an absolute necessity to always commence with your primary keyword. For instance, a Maui Bed and Breakfast website should proceed like the following:

Maui Bed and Breakfast | Sweet Escape Maui

Please note that the primary keyword is the opening phrase. Also note that a "|" instead of a comma or hyphen was used. The preceding segment of the Title Tag is the business name; however, including secondary keywords can be an alternative if you choose. The Title Tag should not be more than 5 to 7 words. *Keyword Prominence* is also a significant factor in determining rank. *Prominence* is how close to the beginning of the section that the keyword is placed. As a general rule, a keyword that is placed closer to the top of the page, near the start of a paragraph, or in close proximity to the commencement of a tag will be more significant. **A Keyword Prominence of at least 64% is suggested for the Title area.** We will accomplish that by putting our primary keyword at the very beginning and by **maintaining a word count of 5 to 7 words**.

Other Recent EzineArticles from the Internet-and-Businesses-Online:SEO Category:

- Tips To Attain Proper Serp's For A Website And Blogsite
- Keywords - How To Optimize Use Of Keywords To Give Your Content Maximum Exposure?
- Online Branding By Way of SEO
- SEO - Search Engine Optimization
- Successful SEO Campaign - 10 Basic Thumb Rules
- Finding Your Keywords For SEO
- Brand New Method To Find Link Exchange Partners
- How To Analyze The Ideal Keyword Density For Web Content Writing?
- Why Google Is Not To Blame Your Lousy Rankings
- Methods To Employ And Avoid in Search Engine Optimization (SEO)
- Link Building Expert In the UK
- Better Search Engine Placement - 3 Ways to Bring Your Site More Exposure Online
- How Do I Increase My Technorati Authority?
- How To Buy Backlinks To Improve Your Rankings
- 5 Steps to SEO Success

(Figure 1.2)

The second most important factor in high search engine rankings is the **anchor text of incoming links,** as illustrated in ***figure 1.2***. The *anchor text* is the evident, clickable text in a hyperlink. The words appearing in the Anchor text can conclude the ranking the site will obtain by search engines. An approach to achieve this crucial step is to acquire incoming links to your site from other websites. Contact topically related sites and exchange links or request that they supply a link on their Links Page. If a site approves your request, then it's imperative that you request that they use your primary keyword as the anchor text. Usually, it is customary to provide the following information when requesting link exchanges:

1. Title of hyperlink. This is the anchor text. Therefore, this is where you want to include your primary keyword within the link title.

2. The URL of the website.

3. The description. You should provide a short, but very concise summary of what your site is about, while including as many important keywords as you can.

4. Also, if you are exchanging links, then you should post the link of the site you are submitting this information to on your Links Page and then let the person know where your Links Page is located so they can verify that you have already placed their link on your site. If you do this, external websites will have extra incentive to link back.

The third most pertinent factor is the **Global Link Popularity of the website**. This is the combined link authority as calculated by links from every single site across the internet, which also includes quality and mass. There are numerous ways to attain high Link Popularity. The best method is to contact as many external websites as you can and request a link exchange as described above. It is also an essential factor to exchange links with topically related websites, that is to say websites that contain similar content. **Always check the PageRank** of the sites you research. Getting your link on high PageRank (preferably PageRank 4 and above) sites is tremendously essential and will be a determining factor in getting high rankings.

Getting top rankings on the search engines is a demanding undertaking that requires hours of work on a weekly basis. It takes time to email other site owners to request a link exchange. It takes time to fully optimize your site; nevertheless, this time will be well spent. Countless people don't comprehend the importance of SEO. They are more concerned about the look and feel of their website. The finest looking website will be utterly useless if it cannot acquire visitors. The only way it can get a vast amount of visitors is to carry out SEO. Since search engines generate over **92%** of all traffic to websites, it would be logical to spend that crucial time working on your keyword rankings.

2

Introduction to
Advanced Search Engine Optimization
Techniques

Merely being listed on the search engines will not mean that customers will discover your product. By understanding precisely how search engines determine who acquires top rankings, we can perform the necessary tasks to achieve that extremely important goal. Getting top rankings on the search engines will result in your site escalating above and beyond the competition, which will, consequently, produce more income and a higher Return on Investment (ROI).

List of most important search engine ranking factors:

1. Keyword Factors:

   a. Keyword Research. Research which keywords are used most often on the search engines. Generate a list of about 10 important keywords and then review the list with site owner before the optimization process begins.
   b. Optimize keyword use within the title tag, body text, H1 tag, domain name, H2 and H3 tags, alt tags, bold/strong tags, META description

tag, META keywords tag, and focus on the keyword density.

2. On-Page Factors:

   a. Validate HTML code to comply with W3C Standards.
   b. Validate CSS code to comply with W3C Standards.
   c. Organizational layout. Proper use of text links and navigational layout to ensure search engine robots and spiders have the opportunity to search all pages throughout the site.
   d. Link popularity. Improve sites like Link Popularity by exchanging links, writing articles related to the service or product that your site offers and getting the article published throughout the web. Finding high PageRank sites to link with, which will greatly increase keyword rankings, etc....
   e. Relevance of links to external sites. Maintain an outbound link structure that focuses on relevant content.
   f. Quality of content. Ensure that the content is properly written and make certain that all the necessary information is provided. Perform technical writing when necessary to improve search engine rankings.
   g. Update pages frequently. It is important to update webpage's frequently with new content. The search engines love sites that have new content on a regular basis.
   h. Spelling and grammar corrections. Ensure that all the text within the site is properly written and spelled correctly.

3. Inbound Link Factors:

   a. Anchor text of inbound link. The anchor text is the evident, clickable text in a hyperlink. An approach to achieve this crucial step is to acquire incoming links to your site from other websites. Contact topically related sites and exchange links or request that they supply a link on their Links Page. If a site approves your request, then it's imperative to request that they use your site's primary keyword as the anchor text.
   b. Global link popularity of linking Site. This is the combined link authority as calculated by links from every single site across the internet, which also includes quality and mass.
   c. Topical relationship of linking Page. One of the most important off-site optimization methods is to exchange links with topically relevant websites. Topically relevant websites are sites that have similar or related content. For example, if you sell shoes online it would be extremely beneficial for you to get a link to your site from another shoe site, or a site that repairs shoes, cleans shoes, and the like. The search engines, especially Google, are including these "relevance" factors in their search algorithms.
   d. Google PageRank of linking page. Another off-site method that is probably the most important off-site search engine optimization factor is to ensure that the linking site has high PageRank, and preferably site's with topical relevance. Your rankings will sky rocket to the very top of the search engines as you continue getting links to your site from high PageRank sites.

4. Website accessibility. Ensure that the site is properly programmed to be compatible with all browsers and operating systems.

5. Get indexed quickly by search engine spiders and crawlers like Googlebot. Ensure that all new sites get indexed in a timely manner by over 300 search engines to speed up the ranking process and to get visitors to your site faster than you would if this essential process was not completed.

6. Directory and Niche directory submissions. Submit your site to internet directories and niche directories across the web to draw the attention of people who are looking for what you have to offer.

7. Search Engine Ranking Reports. Generate monthly reports of site traffic so you can see the amazing progress your site will achieve once you have our advanced search engine optimization performed.

8. Submit your site to search engines on a regular basis.

9. Website Competitive Intelligence. From our expert knowledge about how search engines determine who gets top rankings, we will find out EXACTLY how your top competitors are getting top rankings and determine the steps necessary to have a competitive edge over them.

10. Google Sitemap Creation & Submission. We will create a Google Sitemap and submit it to Google every week, which will assist in accelerated rankings.

11.   Robots.txt optimization. We will create an enhanced robots.txt file which will optimize the way search engines crawl your site.

12.   Proper use of NoIndex and NoFollow Tags. Review each page and determine what links require noindex tags to prevent search engines from following the links that are not beneficial.

13.   Externalizing scripts

14.   Integration/optimization of themed pages (if necessary)

15.   Ongoing Optimization Updates

Other advanced SEO practices

Optimize the sites PDF files to get top rankings. Here are a few ways to accomplish this task:

1. Ensure that the PDF file contains text.

2. Put several links throughout your site that link to the PDF file.

3. Optimize PDF for increased download time.

4. Name the PDF file to match the primary keyword that you desire to optimize and a keyword that relates to the specific PDF file.

5. Submit the PDF file to all the major search engines (optional)

Instead of having a "Home Page" or "Home" link on the bottom of each page, change the title of the link to include a keyword.

Obtain a domain name that contains the primary keyword associated with the particular website, if possible. It is also more beneficial to have dashes between each word in the domain name. Specific web page URLs should also be names to include a specific keyword with dashes between each word.

Include the primary keyword in bold and use an H1 tag. An H2 tag can be used with the second most important keyword. And the H3 tag can be used for the third. Bold and underlining keywords are also beneficial. It is also best to have a link on those keywords that point to the different pages of your website.

Along with including a keyword on the very bottom link section of each page, it is also beneficial to include a keyword at the end of the Body section and also at the very beginning left-hand side of the page.

Advanced Link Building Strategies

Link building involves commitment and persistence. This intricate, extensive and imperative task is essential in getting top rankings. Here's a list of strategies that you can do to build links to a website:

Web Directories

Web Directory submissions are an old tactic that still remains a productive and beneficial method of increasing search engine rankings. There are free directories and paid directories. For an extensive list of Web Directories that include the current fees involved, please see **Directories** in the Glossary section

It is best when submitting to directories to include various anchor text keyword strings to increase the chances of several different keywords becoming optimized for high rankings.

Top Competition

Another strategic approach that always proves to be beneficial is to search the specific keyword rankings that you wish to optimize on all the major search engines. Then contact the site owners of the top ranked sites and request that they link to your site. An email or a direct phone call to the site owner can do the trick. It is also more beneficial to contact the actual owner of the site and not the webmaster since he will be extremely aware that you are their competitors.

Acquiring Competitors' Links

Another imperative approach is to make an extensive list of every site that is linking to your competitors. Then contact those site owners directly to request that they provide a link to your site. There are several methods to locate competitors' link such as:

1. Use the linkdomain:url.com or site:url.com function at Yahoo

2. Also on Yahoo, you can type in link:http://www.url.com

3. Use the link:url.com or site:url.com function at Microsoft Live

4. Type "url.com" or site:url.com at Google

There is also SEO software programs that will find your competitors links, but the methods listed below are usually the easiest and most efficient means.

Writing and Submitting Articles

Writing articles and press releases is also a great means of improving your site's keyword rankings. You can write articles about the site's specific subject matter and submit the articles to online article sites and directories. There are also sites like ezinearticles.com that will syndicate the articles to other websites, so the exposure becomes very extensive. Here's a list of a few article sites that you can submit articles to:

http://www.ezinearticles.com
http://www.amazines.com
http://www.freezinesite.com
http://www.marketing-seek.com
http://www.articlefarm.com
http://www.articlehub.com
http://www.howtoadvice.com
http://www.articlestash.com
http://www.Article-Domain.com
http://www.writeyourarticles.com
http://www.GoArticles.com
http://www.articlesbase.com
http://www.articlesbeach.com
http://www.articlegarden.com
http://www.articlesphere.com
http://www.article99.com
http://www.articlealley.com
http://www.articlesfactory.com
http://www.articlewarehouse.com
http://www.articlecity.com

http://www.webmasterarticles.net
http://www.isnare.com
http://www.ezinearticles.com
http://www.articlehub.com
http://www.valuablecontent.com
http://www.Clickz.com
http://www.BigArticleDirectory.com
http://www.boconline.com/sub-art.shtml
http://www.ActiveArticles.com
http://www.money-articles.com
http://www.content-crazy.com
http://www.websitefuel.com
http://www.cumuli.com/ezines/post.html
http://www.articlehub.com/add.html
http://searchwarp.com/Login.asp
http://www.ArticleCity.com
http://www.warriorforum.com/forum/forum.asp?FORUM_ID=11
http://www.family-content.com/articles/submit.shtml
http://www.netterweb.com/articles/
http://www.webmaster-resources101.com/articles/
http://www.ebooksnbytes.com/articles/submit.shtml
http://www.workoninternet.com/
http://www.ideamarketers.com/
http://www.webpronews.com/submit.html
http://thewhir.com/find/articlecentral/suggest.asp
http://www.xongoo.com/submit.html

Yahoo Announcement Groups:

http://groups.yahoo.com/group/Free_eContent/
http://groups.yahoo.com/group/Free-Reprint-Articles/
http://groups.yahoo.com/group/FreeWrites/
http://groups.yahoo.com/group/freE-zinecontent/
http://groups.yahoo.com/group/netwrite-publish-announce/
http://groups.yahoo.com/group/publisher_network/

http://groups.yahoo.com/group/TheWriteArticles
http://groups.yahoo.com/group/aainet/
http://groups.yahoo.com/group/Free-Content/

The list above are just a few examples of the many article sites that accept submissions. It is also beneficial to find sites related to the specific topic that the article is about. There are many niche article sites as well.

Blogging & Comments

Have a blog and participating in blogs is another great way to increase keyword rankings. Install blog software on the site you are optimizing and begin writing information that contains keywords and attracts the attention of others. You should never spam blog comments with ads or links because that is an unethical approach. The correct approach to benefiting from blogging is to ensure that you comment appropriately & wisely about the particular subject matter in the blog. This intelligent approach will also draw the attention of search engines and visitors to click on your link.

There is the chance that blog links will not get spidered because of NoFollow tags or other forms of link condoms. A little research should determine if a blog is an ideal candidate.

Unique Tools & Services

By contributing particular, pertinent free Internet tools or services on your site, you can produce the accumulation of links that are provided simply by the good will of others. If you site provides useful information, then other sites will have a good reason to provide a link to your site.

Press Releases

Carefully written press releases can be a valuable resource used in the SEO arsenal. Search engines love press releases because they provide fresh content. Press releases will rank exceptionally well the first few days. Here are a few places to submit your press releases:

Free Press Release Services

- PR.com promotion
- PRWeb
- 24-7 Press Release
- PR Leap
- Inewswire
- Press World
- PR Newswire Direct
- AddPR
- PRFree
- Rally Cry List

Paid Press Release Services

PRWeb SEP
Marketwire
Internet News Bureau
Bacon's PR Services
Enewsrelease PR manager

Press releases should be written well, especially if you are releasing important news or information, so it is always best to consider using a professional to write your press releases.

Another tactic to consider is to publish your articles and press releases on your own site, preferably using a blog CMS, and then bookmark all the articles using social bookmarking services and tag them with relevant keywords.

Content syndication is undoubtedly the surefire way to achieve higher rankings and traffic. Here is a list of email addresses of several important newspapers to submit press releases and articles to:

letters@longbeachpress.com
editorial2005@newsfactor.com
letters@linewsday.com
letters@louisvillecourier.com
letters@memphisc-appeal.com
letters@pitssburgpost-gazette.com
letters@providencejournal.com
letters@raleighnewsobservernews.com
letters@richmondtimes.com
letters@rochesterdem.com
letters@rockymtnnews.com
letters@sacramentobee.com
letters@stlouispost.com
letters@stpeterstimes.com
letters@stpaulpioneer.com
letters@saltlaketribune.com
letters@sanantonioexpress-news.com
letters@sandiegounion.com
letters@sfchronicle.com
letters@sfexaminer.com
letters@sanjosemercury
letters@charlestonpostandcourier.com
letters@chicagotribune.com
letters@cincinnatienquirer.com
letters@clarionledger.com
letters@cleplaindealer.com
letters@columbusscstate.com
letters@dallasmorningnews.com

letters@daytondailynews.com
letters@detroitfreepress.com
letters@detroitnews.com
letters@fortworthstar-tele.com
letters@miamiherald.com
letters@milwaukeejournal.com
letters@nydailynews.com
letters@newyorkpost.com
letters@newarkst-ledger.com
letters@norleanspicayune.com
letters@okahoman.com
letters@virginiaport.com
letters@wallstreetjournel.com
letters@wilmingtonnewsjournal.com
letters@worcestertelegram
letters@washingtontimes.com
source-suggestions@google.com
letters@ohahaworld-herald.com
letters@orangecoreg.com
letters@orlandosentinel.com
letters@palmbeachpost.com
letters@sarasotaherald.com
letters@seattlepost.com
letters@seattleposr-intelligencer.com
letters@seattletimes.com
letters@spokanespokesman.com
letters@tacomanewstribune.com
letters@toledoblade.com

Standard Press Release Format

It is always important to make certain that your press release is formatted correctly and looks professional. To achieve this, use the following Stand Press Release Format:

Headline Announces News in Title Case, Ideally Under 80 Characters

The summary paragraph is a little longer synopsis of the news, elaborating on the news in the headline in one to four sentences. The summary uses sentence case, with standard capitalization and punctuation.

City, State (PRWEB) Month 1, 2006 -- The lead sentence contains the most important information in 25 words or less. Grab your reader's attention here by simply stating the news you have to announce. Do not assume that your reader has read your headline or summary paragraph; the lead should stand on its own.

A news release, like a news story, keeps sentences and paragraphs short, about three or four lines per paragraph. The first couple of paragraphs should answer the who, what, when, where, why and how questions. The news media may take information from a news release to craft a news or feature article or may use information in the release word-for-word, but a news release is not, itself, an article or a reprint.

The standard press release is 300 to 800 words and written in a word processing program that checks spelling and grammar before submission to PRWeb. This template is 519 words.

The ideal headline is 80 characters long. PRWeb will accept headlines with a maximum of 170 characters. PRWeb recommends writing your headline and summary last, to be sure you include the most important news elements in the body of the release. Use title case in the headline only, capitalizing every word except for prepositions and articles of three characters or less.

The rest of the news release expounds on the information provided in the lead paragraph. It includes quotes from key staff, customers or subject matter experts. It contains more details about the news you have to tell, which can be about something unique or controversial or about a prominent person, place or thing.

Typical topics for a news release include announcements of new products or of a strategic partnership, the receipt of an award, the publishing of a book, the release of new software or the launch of a new Web site. The tone is neutral and objective, not full of hype or text that is typically found in an advertisement. Avoid directly addressing the consumer or your target audience. The use of "I," "we" and "you" outside of a direct quotation is a flag that your copy is an advertisement rather than a news release.

Do not include an e-mail address in the body of the release. If you do, it will be protected from spambots with a notice to that effect, which will overwrite your e-mail address.

"The final paragraph of a traditional news release contains the least newsworthy material," said Mario Bonilla, member services director for PRWeb. "But for an online release, it's typical to restate and summarize the key points with a paragraph like the next one."

For additional information on the news that is the subject of this release (or for a sample, copy or demo), contact Mary Smith or visit www.prweb.com. You can also include details on product availability, trademark acknowledgment, etc. here.

About XYZ Company:

Include a short corporate backgrounder, or "boilerplate," about the company or the person who is newsworthy before you list the contact person's name and phone number.

Contact:

Mary Smith, director of public relations
XYZ Company
555-555-5555
http://www.prweb.com

###

When will the rankings begin to improve?

Organic Search Engine rankings are optimized by a combination of both On-Page optimization and Off-Page Optimization. You can realistically anticipate escalating keyword results starting four to six weeks following the initial optimization procedure. Rankings usually become stable after approximately two to three months. The duration is calculated from the date of receipt of the SEO

Questionnaire. However, your traffic rises continuously since more and more search engines index more and more optimized pages of your website.

Search Engines are giving increasingly more importance to the off-page factors (external links) in final organic rankings. You will need to invest in a suitable link building campaign for your website (depending on the kind of keywords you wish to rank for) before you can expect to see visible improvement in rankings.

3

Optimizing Keyword Frequencies

The keyword frequencies recommended below are based on the number of times **ANY** of the words in your keyword phrase appear on the page, **DIVIDED** by the number of words in the phrase. The recommendations listed is updated information related to Google as of April, 2008 and may change at anytime. Other search engines may require or suggest different frequencies, but the numbers below are what are suggested to follow.

TITLE KEYWORD FREQUENCY:

A keyword frequency of 1 is suggested for the Title area.

TITLE AREA WORD COUNT:

A word count from 5 to 7 is suggested for the Title area.

TITLE AREA KEYWORD PROMINENCE:

A keyword prominence of at least 64% is suggested for the Title area.

LINK TEXT KEYWORD FREQUENCY:

A keyword frequency from 1 to 13 is suggested for the Link Text area.

LINK TEXT WORD COUNT:

A word count from 1 to 448 is suggested for the Link Text area.

LINK TEXT KEYWORD PROMINENCE:

A keyword prominence of at least 58% is suggested for the Link Text area.

URL KEYWORD FREQUENCY:

A Keyword frequency from 1 to 16 is suggested for the Hyperlink Url area.

BODY TEXT KEYWORD FREQUENCY:

A keyword frequency from 2 to 15 is suggested for the Body Text area.

BODY TEXT WORD COUNT:

A word count from 445 to 615 is suggested for the Body Text area.

BODY TEXT KEYWORD PROMINENCE:

A keyword prominence of at least 62% is suggested for the Body Text area.

TOTAL KEYWORD FREQUENCY:

A total frequency from 5 to 45 is suggested for the page as a whole.

TOTAL PAGE WORD COUNT:

A total word count from 468 to 912 is suggested for the page as a whole.

ALT TEXT KEYWORD FREQUENCY:

A keyword frequency from 1 to 2 is suggested for the Alt area.

ALT TAG WORD COUNT:

A word count from 1 to 64 is suggested for the Alt area.

ALT TAG KEYWORD PROMINENCE:

A keyword prominence of at least 57% is suggested for the Alt area.

KEYWORD SELECTION

Google now uses word stemming technology, is a process now implemented by Google and other search engines that search keywords as well as any variations of the keyword. One way to benefit from this is to search for your keyword phrase in both the singular and plural versions in Google. If the results are equivalent, then use WordTracker to decide which version has the most potential for traffic with the smallest amount of competitors.

4

Topical Relevance

Search Engine Optimization will always remain the most vital website promotion and marketing method. Search Engine algorithms establish which factors determine the sites that obtain top rankings. These algorithms are relentlessly altering which is the reason search engine results are continuously changing. Understanding how search engines work by learning about the fundamental aspects of search engine optimization can give your website the utmost potential for unremitting exposure and high rankings. Because search engines generate over 90% of traffic to all websites, it becomes evident that achieving top rankings should be a site owner's top objective. On-site optimization such as proper META Tag content, keyword use in the body text, keyword use in H1, H2, and H3 tags, proper navigational structure using text links, etc... is very important in achieving top rankings; however, off-site optimization is equally, if not more, important. In this article, I will discuss the most important off-site optimization factors, especially the importance of topical relevance.

One of the most important off-site optimization methods is to exchange links with topically relevant websites. Topically relevant websites are sites that have similar or related content. For example, if you sell shoes online it would be extremely beneficial for you to get a link to your site from another shoe site, or a site that repairs shoes, cleans shoes, and the like. The search engines, especially

Google, are including these "relevance" factors in their search algorithms. Because of this, all site owners should thoroughly search for and request link exchanges with topically relevant sites.

Another off-site method that is probably the most important off-site search engine optimization factor is to ensure that the linking site has high PageRank, and preferably site's with topical relevance. Your rankings will sky rocket to the very top of the search engines as you continue getting links to your site from high PageRank sites. Constantly confirm the PageRank of the sites you investigate. Getting your link on high PageRank (preferably PageRank 4 and over) sites is extremely imperative and will be an influential aspect in getting high rankings.

Not only is topical relevance and high PageRank site linking important, but another essential factor is incorporating your primary keyword as the anchor text in the hyperlink. . The *anchor text* is the evident, clickable text in a hyperlink. For this reason, drop a line to topically related sites and exchange links or ask if they could provide a link on their Links Page. If a site approves your request, then it's imperative that you request that they use your primary keyword as the anchor text. A short description with your primary keyword and a few additional keywords would also be helpful.

The off-site optimization factors listed above just scratch the surface. Explaining the others will require several more articles because the list is extensive; however, I will provide you with the basics so you can prepare for a successful search engine optimization journey. First, what is **Off-page Optimization**? Off-page optimization refers to factors that have an outcome on your website ranking in natural search results directly associated with outside circumstances. The most important examples of off-page optimization include the following:

- The amount of websites linking to you
- The PageRank and Link Popularity of the websites linking to you
- Topical relevance of the sites linking to you
- Link popularity of site in topical community
- The Anchor Text used in the links linking to you
- Whether or not the websites linking to you are considered an authority website.
- The Page Title of the websites linking to you
- The amount and quality of links linking to the website that's linking to you
- The total amount of links on the website that is linking to you
- The quantity of outbound links on the website that is linking to you
- Directory Submissions
- Creating proper robot.txt
- Google Sitemap Creation & Submission
- And many, many more factors

When beginning the search engine optimization process, always remember that off-site optimization is vitally important in achieving top search engine rankings. Focus considerable time locating link partners from topically relevant websites. Also, keep in mind that contacting high PageRank sites to exchange links would be the most efficient and profitable approach.

5

Search Engine Optimization
Advanced Glossary

301 Redirect

is a permanent server redirect that instructs Web browsers to view a different URL from the one the browser requested. This process is employed when a web page has permanently moved to a new URL. Employing a 301 Redirect is the most favored technique of redirecting for a good number of web pages or websites. Your site authority rating or the frequency your site is crawled may determine the amount of time it will take for the 301 redirect to be implemented.

302 Redirect

is a temporary redirect or "found" message. This method of redirection is typically used when a URL has been relocated to a new URL. Additionally, the URL will eventually move back for this is only a temporary redirect. It is best to avoid using 302 Redirects when at all possible because several search engines resist this form of redirect.

403 Server Code

is a "forbidden" message. A 403 Server Code inhibits access to a URL and will show the cause of the disturbance and why it is not allowing access.

404 Server Code

is a "not found" message. In this case, the server was incapable of locating the URL.

A

Adwords

(Figure 5.1)

is a Google Pay Per Click (PPC) contextual advertisement program. Adwords is now becoming an extremely common means of essential website advertisement. Google AdWords ads are displayed on the right side and very top of the search results page, as illustrated in *figure 5.1*. The majority of Google's ads is targeted toward keywords and is purchased on a cost-per-click (CPC) basis. Google Adwords is becoming tremendously popular with site owners and marketing specialists because of the exposure the ads generate. Google Adwords is also expanding to include other types of ads like video ads, etc....Google Adwords is a very complex marketplace and will expand as the Internet Superhighway continues to expand.

Affiliate Marketing

is a marketing procedure of revenue sharing that permits merchants to replicate sales efforts by joining efforts. In an affiliate marketing program, the affiliates receive a referral payment, based on clicks or by a cost-per-action (CPA) basis. On average, niche affiliate sites make more money from affiliate marketing because niche markets are easier to focus on.

Algorithm (algo or "secret sauce")

is a code of behavior that search engine use to rank listings contained within its index, in response to a particular query. Search engines protect their algorithms strictly because they are the distinctive blueprint used to establish relevancy; and, to protect itself from competitors and those spamming the search engine.

Alt Text (alternative text or alt attribute)

is an HTML tag (ALT tag) founded to supply images with a text description in the event images are turned off in a web browser. You can visually see the ALT tag text by hovering your mouse over an image in Internet Explorer. Other browsers like Firefox may not display the ALT tag content. In SEO terms, Alt text is significant because search engines do not view the actual images, just the Alt text. Consequently, a popular way to optimize images is to put primary keywords in the Alt text (without keyword stuffing). Additionally, special web browsers for visually impaired individuals entrust the alt text to make the content of images unrestricted to the users.

Analytics

is a procedure which analyzes and accumulates information about website usage. Google analytics is a valuable, mainstream, free program to use.

Anchor Text

is the evident, clickable text in a hyperlink. Anchor text is utilized by search engines to indicate relevance for that web page. Search engines theorize the importance and give authority for the words that people include in the anchor text pointing to your site. The words appearing in the Anchor text can conclude the ranking the site will obtain by search engines. A method of obtaining high rankings is to include your primary keywords in the anchor text like the following:

Example of anchor text:

<a href="http://americreations.com">Search Engine Optimization Expert</a>

Authority (trust or Google juice)

is the measure of trust a site is given for a certain keyword search. Authority is influenced from relevant inbound linking from other authority sites. Other factors include the age of site, traffic and website history, and the uniqueness and quality of the site's content. Search engines generally distinguish outstanding importance on websites that contain an abundance of links from other websites that have many incoming links, and rank those websites at the top of the search engines for keywords related to subjects that are topically related.

Authority Site

is a site which has an abundance of inbound links from other topically authoritative websites. Ebay is a good example of an authority website. Authority sites typically have high PageRank and top search engine rankings.

B

Backlink (inlink, incoming or inbound link)

is a link pointing to one website from another website. You may view the backlinks, both incoming and internal links, by using the link: function on a search engine. Google usually does not display the quantity of links that other search engines like Yahoo or MSN, so if you desire to use this method, it would be best to use Yahoo or MSN and not Google. Additionally, although Google doesn't visually display the incoming and internal links to a site using the link: function, Google does, on the other hand, recognize most of the links that are present on sites.

Black hat SEO

is "unethical" search engine optimization practices and the complete opposite of "White Hat SEO," which is a set of "guidelines" that search engines set forth for webmasters to adhere to. If these guidelines, or "ethical" tactics, are followed, then a website should not get penalized or banned by a search engine. These guidelines change from one day to the next, so all SEO specialists should continually "keep up with the times" to avoid getting a site penalized or banned for potentially unethical techniques. However, these guidelines are not actually a static set of rules and can change without notice. Search engines make these guidelines to generate billions of dollars by keeping internet marketers paying them for advertisements. On the other hand, search engines like Google do try their best to stay fair and "ethical" themselves. here is a list of some of current Black Hat SEO tactics:

Keyword Stuffing
Cloaking
Invisible Text
Doorway Page
Spam Page
Interlinking
Selling PageRank
Buying Expired Domains
Submission software
Adding links on their own websites
Link dealers
Submission in thousands search engines / directories
 "Sneaky redirects"
Trademark infringement
Duplicating content

Pagejacking
Participating in link farms
Blog comment spamming
Guestbook spamming

Blog

is a website which chronologically displays information. A majority of blogs use Content Management Systems (CMS) like WordPress or something similar. Blogs resemble periodically revised journals, and are typically presented in reverse chronological order. Because the majority of blogs use a Content Management System, they provide interactive features such as allowing comments, polls, feedback, and so forth. Furthermore, Blogs have a tendency to categorize the content for unproblematic navigation and layout. Blogs are primarily personal in nature. Because blogs are updated on a regular basis, they tend to generate high link equity so blogs are a popular means for escalating PageRank and high rankings if used appropriately.

Blogs and blog posts are naturally search engine friendly because they contain fresh content, many links, and regularly revised web pages.

If you adhere to some basic guidelines when optimizing blogs and blog posts, the search engine rankings may have a much better change of acquiring higher rankings than static web pages. Here are a few basic guidelines to follow:

1. **Use your primary keyword in your blog domain**

   Ensure that the url of the blog contains a primary keyword, whether acquiring a separate domain or if you locate the blog in a sub-domain of your site.

2. **Incorporate the principal keyword in the blog header tags and the title of a majority, if not all, of the posts**

   For example, if your blog pertains to SEO Tactics, then it is preferable to include the keyword SEO and Tactics in the domain or url of the blog.

3. **In the body of your posts, it is beneficial to incorporate the secondary keyword**

   Always remember when making blog posts that you want to make sure that the post sound natural if you use keyword phrases. If they don't, then the posts could get removed on other blog sites.

4. **Incorporate your keywords in the Anchor Text of the links in the blog and blog posts**

5. **Ensure that the blog has great spiderability**

   You always want to make sure that all old posts are archived and accessible from all the other pages so they can continually get spidered by the search engines.

6. **Acquire backlinks from other sites and blogs**

7. **Regularly update the blog**

Search engines greatly prefer blogs that get updated frequently, so always try to add new content on a regular basis to keep the search engine and the blog readers happy.

Bookmarking

is a way to keep track of your favorite websites, web pages, articles, forums, or other content. Bookmarks increase the popularity of a webpage or document if it's bookmarked by many people. It also becomes a way for many web-based services to give authority to information. Many sites may feature heavily bookmarked information on their Home Page or Featured Page. There are also Social Bookmarking sites like Del.icio.us, Digg, and Netscape to name a few. For more information, please see *Social Bookmarking*.

Bot (robot, crawler, or spider)

is a program that runs autonomously that is designed to handle a particular procedure. Bots are used by search engines to search out and find web pages to populate their index. Bots are also used by spammers to gather information for use in email spam. When bots search a web page, they seek out the readable text on a page, starting from the top left of a web page, and they work their way down to the bottom right. They do not view images, except for the ALT tag information. Because of this, it is extremely important to have actual text on a web page with primary keywords so the bots can access the information for their search index.

Bounce Rate

is the percentage of visitors to a website who open a website and then leave without opening any other pages within that particular website. A low Bounce Rate symbolizes quality and interesting content.

Bread Crumbs

is a navigational layout used by users and search engines to comprehend the organization of a website. Bread crumbs can also assist in helping a visitor find his/her way back to other areas of the site and exactly how to return back to the Home Page. Here is an example:

Home > Search Engine Optimization Services > SEO Glossary

As you can see from the example, web pages are linked in order starting with the Home Page.

Broken Link

is a hyperlink that's out of action. In other words, a broken link is a link that does not direct the user or search engine to a specified location. Search engines and users do not appreciate broken links. Many circumstances may result in a broken link. For instance, if a website were to go down, then a broken link would occur to any external link pointing to that particular web page. Broken links often occur when temporary content is made available. Other factors may also result in a broken link like changing the organizational structure of a website by changing the e-commerce software or Content Management System (CMS). To avoid potential broken links, always try to analyze the web page and its content to confirm that it will remain and not go offline for whatever reason. There are also web tools available and software programs that can check your site for broken links.

C

Cache

in terms of SEO, is a copy of a web page that search engines "stash" or store to keep in their index until they update it. Search engine bots (robots, spiders, and crawlers) store the results in the search engine index so a user can locate the contents of a particular web page. The stored information is not updated on a regular basis, and can be outdated if a particular website is not crawled regularly.

Canonical Issues

or duplicate content, is caused because www.americreations.com, americreations.com, and www.americreations.com/index.html are all the same thing and are seen by the search engines as duplicate content. Content Management Systems are notorious for these problems; however, there are ways to solve these canonical issues. One method of solving the issue is to employ a 301 Server Redirect to the "canon", or official version. Another method is to use a noindex html tag on the non-canonical versions. A way for search engines

41

to determine which page is the official or canonical version is to implement PageRank or something similar. Web developers should always implement consistent navigational layouts throughout the site to guarantee that they direct the search engine bots to the canonical version to produce the highest possible PageRank to the URLs they wish the search engines to continually index.

Cascading Style Sheets or CSS

permit you to manage the layout and appearance of your page with ease. CSS tags or properties are comprehensible and influence the appearance, experience, or style of your web pages. A Cascading Style Sheet (CSS) is a list of rules that can designate a variety of rendering properties to HTML elements. Style rules can be given for a solitary element, multiple elements, a complete web page or document, or even several documents at the same time. Style sheets permit an extensive amount of layout and display control. The amount of format coding necessary to control display characteristics can be greatly reduced through the use of external style sheets which can be used by a group of documents. Cascading Style Sheets are a gigantic advancement in web design because they permit designers to regulate the style and layout of multiple web pages in a flash. Without Style Sheets, a webmaster would have to change styles and layouts on each individual page if changes were needed. Cascading Style Sheets function similar to a template and allow web designers to classify styles and assign them to one or many pages. Here is a list of general CSS commands:

BOXES:

margin
margin-top
margin-right
margin-bottom
margin-left
padding
padding-top
padding-right
padding-bottom
padding-left
border
border-top
border-bottom
border-right
border-left
border-color
border-top-color
border-right-color
border-bottom-color

PAGING:

size
marks
page-break-before
page-break-after
page-break-inside
page
orphans
widows

COLOR/BACKGROUND:

color
background
background-color
background-image
background-repeat
background-attachment
background-position

FONTS:

font
font-family
font-style
font-variant
font-weight
font-stretch
font-size
font-size-adjust

TEXT:

text-indent
text-align
text-decoration
text-shadow
letter-spacing
word-spacing
text-transform

border-
left-color

border-
style

border-
top-style

border-
right-style

border-
bottom-
style

border-
left-style

border-
width

border-
top-width

border-
right-
width

border-
bottom-
width

border-
left-width

POSITIO NING:

display

position

top

right

bottom

left

float

clear

z-index

white-space

TABLES:

caption-side

table-layout

border-collapse

border-spacing

empty-cells

speak-header

INTERFACE:

cursor

outline

outline-width

outline-style

outline-color

AURAL:

volume

speak

pause

pause-before

pause-after

cue

cue-before

cue-after

play-during

azimuth

elevation

speech-rate

voice-family

pitch

pitch-range

stress

richness

speak-punctuation

speak-numeral

direction
unicode-
bidi
overflow
clip
visibility

**DIMENSI
ONS:**
width
min-width
max-
width
height
min-
height
max-
height
line-
height
vertical-
align

MISC:
content
quotes
counter-
reset
counter-
increment
marker-
offset
list-style
list-style-
type
list-style-
image

list-style-
position

Click Fraud

is a method of profit that's not deserved that is
usually employed by the publisher or subordinates
and is acquired by improper clicks on a Pay Per
Click (PPC) advertisement. Google and other
advertisement agencies despise this problem
because It reduces the trust of advertisers because
click fraud can raise the costs of people who use
AdWords, Yahoo Search Marketing, or similar
agencies.

Click-Through

is when a website visitor clicks on a hyperlink and is
taken to the link's destination point.

Click-Through Rate

is a percentage of users who click on a link
compared to the amount of users who see the link.
In other words, if 100 people do a web search and
20 people choose one particular link to click on,
then that particular link has a 20% click-through
rate. Click-through rates is also a good method of
calculation in determining user preferences.

Cloaking

is the act of displaying different content to the
search engine bots than that noticeable by the real
user. This process can get a site banned from a
search engine and is considered a Black Hat SEO
technique. Additionally, there are some acceptable

cloaking strategies such as changing content based on location.

Code Swapping, or "bait and switch"

is the process of altering site content after achieving top search engine rankings.

Competitive Analysis

in regards to SEO, is the process of acquiring and evaluating the positive and negative attributes of competing sites. Competitive analysis also includes recognizing traffic patterns, advertising and marketing techniques, and keyword use.

Here's a list of items that should be analyzed when conducting Competitive Analysis:

1. **Page Titles**

   Analyze your competitors' Page Titles. Do they vary or change? What keywords are they focusing on? What is the Keyword Density of the Page Titles? How words do they use?

2. **META Tags**

   Do your competitors have META Description tags that vary from page to page? Analyze all aspects of the META tags to learn more about their approach.

3. **Content Quality**

   Do your competitors use the same information over and over on the different web pages of their site? What kind of content are they providing and how much? How many keywords are they using within that content?

4. Robots.txt File

Analyze their robots.txt file to determine what they are instructing the search engines to do. Then analyze the reasoning behind that.

5. Link Building

How many sites are linking to your competition? What anchor text is used with the backlinks? What is the PageRank of each backlink? What methods do they seem to use to acquire links?

6. Saturation

How many web pages of your competitors site has been indexed with the search engines?

7. Site Design, Architecture and Technology

Is the site design functional and user-friendly? Do they use a text navigational layout? Is the site SEO friendly? Is the site professionally designed?

8. Rankings

What keywords are your competitors using and what are their rankings?

How you can benefit and utilize the information you collect

Once you determine everything listed above, you can begin to make your site better than your competition in every way. If your competitor only has 100 backlinks, then make it your goal to gain 200 or 20,000. If your competitor only has a backlink on 1 PageRank 6 website, then make it a point to get your link on more or even a PageRank 7 website, and so forth.

Content

is the text on a web page or document and is provided to the user as a source of information.

Content Management System (CMS)

are programs that automatically "manage" content. They are very beneficial to a web designer because once a Content Management System is properly setup, it will basically run itself. Some examples of Content Management Systems are PHP-Nuke, Post-Nuke, WordPress, and Joomla to name a few. Here is a detailed list of current Content Management Systems:

Ariadne	MODx CMS
Arti Velocity 3	NitroTech
b2evolution	NPDS
BlogCMS	Nucleus CMS
Categorizator	OpenPHPNuke
C-Arbre	phpBB
Caravel CMS	Phortail
Chlorine Boards	PHP Director
Chrono-Site	PHP-Fusion

Cwiab
CMSimple
CMS Made Simple
Coppermine
CuteNews
DBHcms
DotClear
DokuWiki
Drigg
Drupal
e107
eGroupWare
Exponent
eZ publish
Freeglobes
Geeklog
GuppY
IntraLibre
Itseasy
Jaws
Joomla!
Kwiki
Lemon CMS
Lodel
Lyceum
Mambo
MediaWiki
Midgard CMS

PHPMotion
PHP-Nuke
Phpdug
PHPList
PhpMyFaq
phpWCMS
phpWebSite
phpCMS
PhpWiki
Pivot
Pligg
PmWiki
PortalPHP
PostNuke
PunBB
PuzzleApps
SMF
SNews
Spip
Templeet
Textpattern
TikiWiki
Typo3
Wikini
Wordpress
Xaraya
YACS
Xoops

Content Rich

is quality information (text) that is composed of thorough and pertinent content of a specific topic. A search engine's primary objective is to provide users with the most content rich sites for each keyword. Content rich specifically means high quality, relevant content.

Contextual Advertisement (content inventory)

is when advertisements are displayed on web pages where the advertisements are relevant or related to the page's content. The ad-server analyzes a web page and determines the best "match" in relation to certain keywords on that page. A great example of Contextual Advertisements is Google's AdWords and AdSense ad networks. An example of contextual ads would be when an Ink Cartridge ad would be displayed on a web page that has content about printer repair.

Conversion

is obtaining or accomplishing a measurable objective. In terms of SEO, conversions can be obtained by establishing a goal to receive a certain amount of traffic, click-throughs, or sales.

Conversion Rates

are calculations that determine the amount of users who follow through with a particular action. Conversion rates are typically a percentage. For example, if your preferred action step is to sell one special product, and if you had 20 visitors and only 2 bought that product, then the Conversion Rate would be 10%. To calculate conversion rates follow this simple formula:

Total click-throughs that perform the desired action, divided by the total number of click-throughs for that advertisement or link.

To achieve a high ROI (Return on Investment) and a thriving Pay Per Click (PPC) campaign, you should focus on achieving a high conversion rate.

CPC (Cost Per Click)

is the amount of money spent per click for a Pay Per Click advertiser. Pay Per Click advertisers require you to pay a certain amount per click for a desired keyword or ad. Google AdWords is an example of a Pay Per Click advertiser and to use this service, you would have to bid on a Cost Per Click amount to pay for each advertisement campaign. You will then have to pay Google the agreed upon bid amount every time someone clicks on your ad.

CPM (Cost Per Thousand Impressions)

the "M" in "CPM" stands for the Roman Numeral for One Thousand. CPM is used to calculate the average cost or value of Pay Per Click advertisements.

Crawler (robot or spider)

is a program that directs its way throughout the web or website to gather information to display in a search engine index. Crawlers navigate throughout the web or website by following link structures. A crawler reads text on a web page and the ALT text of images, but not the images themselves.

D

Deep Linking

is linking that directs users and search engines to a specific page at a different website, but not directly linking to the Home Page. Deep linking occurs from PPC advertisements and from search engines.

Description Tag

is a META Tag that contains a web page's description for the search engines. Most search engines display the content of the META Description Tag directly after the Hyperlink when searching.

Directory, or Web Directory

Web directories have existed before any of the current search engines like Google. Web Directories are databases of web pages that are categorized for easy navigation. Web Directories often contain thousands or even more sites. Usually, there are several different general and sometimes sub-categories to choose from. Like search engines, Web Directories offer a search feature so a user can locate the information they request.

Most Web Directories have human editors, so the editors ensure that the sites are located in the correct categories. Most Web Directories do charge either a one-time fee or a yearly fee. These fees do vary between the various directories.

Here is a detailed list of Directories:

http://www.dmoz.org/
http://dir.yahoo.com
http://www.business.com/
http://botw.org/
http://bubl.ac.uk/
http://directory.v7n.com
http://www.ezilon.com/
http://www.iwebtool.com/directory/
http://www.2yi.net/
http://www.dirjournal.com/
http://www.goguides.org/
http://www.webworldindex.com/
http://www.allinfodir.com/
http://www.avivadirectory.com/
http://www.blazemp.com/dir/
http://www.busybits.com/
http://www.domaining.in/
http://www.elib.org/
http://www.familyfriendlysites.com/
http://www.gii.in/
http://www.gimpsy.com/
http://www.index-it.net/
http://www.joeant.com/
http://www.mozdex.com/directory/
http://www.mygreencorner.com/
http://www.relmaxtop.com/
http://www.romow.com/
http://www.skaffe.com/
http://www.tygo.com/dir
http://www.uncoverthenet.com/
http://www.vxbox.com/
http://www.alivedirectory.com/
http://www.allydirectory.com/
http://blogannounce.info/
http://www.bloggeries.com/

http://www.BlogTagstic.com/
http://www.browse8.com/
http://www.cascandra.com/
http://www.ebjuris.com/
http://www.e-topic.com/directory/
http://www.qoobe.org/
http://www.incrawler.com/
http://www.kahuki.com/
http://www.linkopedia.com/
http://www.linksjuice.com/
http://www.makeasearch.com/
http://www.map100.com/
http://www.onlinewide.com/
http://www.platinax.co.uk/directory/
http://www.prolinkdirectory.com/
http://www.sevenseek.com/
http://www.site-sift.com/
http://www.szab.net/
http://www.uksmallbusinessdirectory.co.uk/
http://www.ventedoy.com/
http://www.wowdirectory.com/
http://www.123kidzarea.com/
http://9ug.com/
http://www.abilogic.com/
http://www.anthonyparsons.com/
http://www.apahcinc.org/
http://ask-dir.com/
http://www.authoritydirectory.com/
http://www.bigweblinks.com/
http://www.blogaboutmysite.com/directory
http://www.citystar.com/
http://www.dirarchive.com/
http://www.directorydump.com/
http://www.elegantdirectory.com/
http://www.emillie.net/
http://www.global-weblinks.com/
http://www.haabaa.com/

http://www.homesalez.com/directory/
http://www.idk.in/
http://www.kwikgoblin.com/
http://www.nobledirectory.com/
http://www.nzpages.co.nz/
http://www.pegasusdirectory.com/
http://www.photarium.com/
http://www.postdotcom.com/
http://www.qango.com/
http://www.rakcha.com/
http://www.searchbuster.org/
http://www.searchnlink.com/
http://www.seoma.net/
http://www.submission4u.com/
http://www.web10.ws/
http://www.webahead.net/
http://www.web1directory.com/
http://www.webotopia.org/
http://www.webs-best-directory.com/
http://www.wezp.com/
http://www.aerospect.com/
http://www.alikedirectory.com/
http://www.all4seo.net/
http://www.arcadeforce.com/
http://www.argusvision.net/
http://www.bakie.com/
http://www.beaconpost.com/
http://www.businessseek.biz/
http://www.cbravo.com/
http://www.cdhnow.com/
http://www.deeplink.us/
http://www.directorymix.com/
http://www.dirwizard.com/
http://www.easyfinddirectory.com/
http://www.ebusiness-directory.com/
http://www.enquira.com/
http://www.ensuredirectory.com/

http://www.eonte.com/
http://www.ewebpages.org/
http://www.excellentguide.com/
http://www.fullofsearch.com/
http://www.freewebindex.com/
http://www.frogengine.com/search
http://www.goongee.com/
http://www.highstuff.com/
http://www.linkcentre.com/
http://www.link-pimp.com/
http://www.linkspub.com/
http://www.linkwith.us/
http://www.massivelinks.com/
http://www.maxdirectory.eu/
http://www.maxlinks.org/
http://www.mingleon.com/
http://www.premiumdir.com/
http://www.search4i.com/
http://www.top5jamaica.com/
http://www.umdum.com/

Directory Page

refs to a web page that contains links that are related to web pages and resources. Directory pages may also be referred to as Links Page, Resources Page, Cool Links, My Friends, Recommended Links, and so on.

Doorway

or gateway, is a web page that has the purpose of drawing traffic from a search engine.

Dynamic Content

consists of a web page that is generated immediately as the user views it. The content delivered to the user is frequently restructured instantly out of a database or based upon the users browser. Search engines no longer penalize for dynamic content providing the URL does not contain submitted data

Dynamic Landing Pages

are non-static or changeable web pages where click-through users are sent that contains specific content which is related to the specific keyword search that was conducted.

E

E-Commerce

is a website whose primary purpose is to sell retail products. E-commerce websites are basically online stores that sell products, services, or information. E-Commerce is becoming more and more popular because business owners are discovering that they can work from home and sell their products or services directly from an e-commerce site. E-commerce benefits all businesses because it enables a wider customer-base and expands their product or service not only to everyone locally, but also everyone around the world.

Email Marketing

is advertising that promoting products or services through email.

Entry Page, please see Landing Page.

Ethical SEO

is search engine optimization techniques that conform to search engine guidelines and best practices. Another term for Ethical SEO is "White Hat SEO". Ethical SEO is just as it implies, ethical. There are no deceptive or underground techniques used to manipulate search engine results. It is always most desirable to apply Ethical SEO practices so that your website will not get banned or penalized for disobeying the search engine best practice guidelines. Here's a list of what NOT TO DO to conduct Ethical SEO:

Perform procedures that will harm your client or their rankings. Specifically, Black Hat SEO tactics should not be used in any way.

Knowingly conduct in practices that go against search engine guidelines.

Knowingly perform in tasks that violate your client's confidentiality.

Violate copyright or trademark laws or any other internet related laws.

Neglect to perform regular search engine optimization updates and optimization practices. Search engine optimization is an ongoing process and should be treated as such.

F

Feeds

is information that is produced to a user by way of
news or informational websites. Feeds are content
that is a version of a web page that becomes
syndicated for wide distribution to all those who
desire to display the content. Feeds are typically
produced from a subscription by a user. There are
also ad feeds that are released to shopping engines
and similar sites. Most feeds, especially ad feeds,
are XML (Extensible Markup Language) or RSS
(Rich Site Summary) format.

FFA

or "Free for All," is a web page or website that
contains a general directory of links with no specific
purpose and no unique information. Free for All
sites, or Link Farms, are frown upon by the search
engines and are considered on unethical or Black
Hat SEO tactic because its primary purpose is to
get crawled by the search engines and does not
benefit the user by containing unique or original
content. Free for All web pages take submissions
and usually runs itself. This is an old and outdated
technique that was originally used to increase link
popularity and PageRank.

Frame

is a web page layout where different, more than
one, frames are used to display separate content.
In terms of SEO, frames are a terrible technique to
utilize because search engine crawlers rarely

properly navigate them, thereby missing pertinent information altogether. Users also despise the use of frames because they are difficult to function and navigate and often become confusion and irritating to users. Webmasters should never use frames if they wish to get high keyword rankings because spiders usually only search one of the frames and miss the others.

G

Gateway Page (doorway page)

is a web page that has the purpose of drawing traffic from a search engine and then rerouting the search engine to a different website or web page. A gateway or doorway page is similar but different than cloaking but the general idea is similar: produce users and search engines different content.

Gizmo (gadget or widget)

are functions employed on web pages to enable certain features like displaying weather, a clock, a hit counter, and so similar functions.

Geo-Targeting

is the process of concentrating on demographic locations when conducting an advertising campaign. Geo-targeting enables one to restrict ad placements to only display to areas of a specific geographic location. This process produces an enhanced ad campaign by localizing and personalizing the ads. Most ad agencies such as

Google and Yahoo allow advertisers to target specific geographic locations such as countries, states, or cities.

Google Juice (PageRank, Authority, or Trust)

is authority (trust) from Google that follows links to other web pages.

Googlebot

is the spider program implemented by Google. Googlebot is surely the most recognized spider or robot program employed by a search engine.

GYM

refers to Google, Yahoo, and Microsoft Live Search (formally know as MSN Search), which is undoubtedly the largest and most influential search engines operating on the web today.

H

.htaccess

is a configuration directive file that is placed in a website file directory which applies to the specific file directory that it gets placed in and all subdirectories therein.

Hit

is an outdated method of determining website traffic. Hits are now irrelevant because every time a web page opens, a "hit" would occur when the page itself opens, and also 1 hit would be calculated for each object or image within that web page. A more useful and accurate method of calculating user traffic to a web page would be to calculate Page Views.

Hub (authority or expert page)

is an authoritative/trusted web page or site that contains valuable, relevant content and links to topically related sites.

HTML (Hyper Text Markup Language)

is a web code or directive (markup) that is used to manage formatting, layout, and style to a web page to be displayed on the web. Search engines prefer HTML to crawl so webmasters should focus on containing properly formatted and validated HTML code on web pages to achieve top rankings. Every webmaster should validate the HTML code on each web page, especially the Home Page because more value is always given to a site's Home Page. Also, webmasters should adhere to the standard's set forth by W3C, which is The World Wide Web Consortium who develops interoperable technologies to guide the Internet to its utmost potential. By validating the HTML code, we are assuring that the HTML is properly written, which will, in turn, keep the search engines happy. Validated HTML pages will also be more accessible to the wide range of Internet browsers, monitors, and operating systems used today.

Hyperlink

is a text-string or graphical element that contains a link to another web page. Therefore, when a user clicks on a hyperlink, they will be directed to a different web page.

I

Impression or Page View

is a method of accurately tracking traffic to a web page. Every impression occurs for each time a user views a web page or advertisement. Impressions are the means that ad agencies use to calculate the amount of times a user clicked through an ad to go to it's specific location.

Inbound Links (Incoming or Inlink)

are links pointing to a website which draws users to that specific location. Inbound links coming from relevant or related web pages is a great method of SEO tactics that will produce high PageRank and trust.

Index (noun)

is used by search engines to store the content of web pages into a database.

Index (verb)

is the act of adding a web page into a search engines index.

Indexability (Spiderability or Crawlability)

refers to a web page whose contents can get potentially crawled by search engines. For example, text on a web page is indexable, but the images and components usually are not. Search engines are finally beginning to index the contents of a web page built entirely in Flash; however, if you desire high search engine rankings, then it is always best to have static html text in a web page for the search engines to crawl.

Indexed Page

is a web page or pages that are currently residing in a search engine's index. It is always desirable to get most, if not all, of a site's pages indexed so keywords within their content can have the potential to get high or noticeable rankings.

K

Keyword, or Key Phrase

is the string of word(s) or a phrase that users enter in a search field to access the search engines relevant content. For example, a user seeking to invest in a new website would type in "Web Design", "Web Designer", "Website Design", or a more specific keyword like "Maui Web Design" or "Maui Website Design" to target web designers in a certain geographic location. As you can see from this one example, there are many possible keyword variations that a user may type in a search engine. Because of this, it is extremely important for a webmaster or marketer to conduct Keyword Analysis when optimizing the site for top rankings. There are web tools available and software that can calculate how many times a particular keyword was used on a search engine per month. You would then research every variation of possible keywords for a specific type of website. You would then determine the most important keyword and then create a list of all other important keywords. You would then optimize the primary keyword(s) to achieve top search engine rankings.

Keyword Analysis

as explained directly above, is the process of analyzing all the variations of a keyword or key phrase and then determine which keyword or keywords are most important. A search engine optimization specialist would then focus on optimizing primary keywords for high rankings.

It is true and well-known that different keywords rank differently because of the competition. It is ordinary for websites to rank extremely high for one particular keyword but not very well for another. This is because of keyword competition and how many competing websites are optimizing the same keyword

Accumulating Information

You should gather the following data when conduct Keyword Analysis:

1. How many web pages use all the words of a specific key phrase?
2. How many web pages on the site uses an exact keyword/key phrase?
3. How many web pages does the site use the keyword or key phrase in the Page Title?
4. How many backlinks does the site have?

There are several methods to locate competitors' link such as:

a. Use the linkdomain:url.com or site:url.com function at Yahoo

b. Also on Yahoo, you can type in link:http://www.url.com

c. Use the link:url.com or site:url.com function at Microsoft Live

d. Type "url.com" or site:url.com at Google

After you have finished the Keyword Analysis process, you can put all the data into a spreadsheet for easy viewing and organization. Once you determine everything listed above, you can begin to make your site better than your competition by outdoing their tactics.

Keyword Cannibalization

is the repeated use of a keyword within the same website. This technique is not a good method to adhere to because search engines find it difficult to determine which web page is most relevant to a specific keyword. Keyword Cannibalization could get you penalized because search engines do not like this practice.

Keyword Density

is the ratio of a keyword or key phrase on a page in relation to all other keywords on that page. If a particular keyword is repeatedly used on a web page, then that keyword will have a higher density compared to all the other words that appear on the page. For example, if you have a 500 word page and your specific keyword is repeated 50 times, then the keyword density of that page would be 10% for that specific keyword. A good rule of thumb to consider when optimizing a web page is that search engines typically regard a web page with a 6 to 8% keyword density a high quality page for that keyword or key phrase. If the keyword density is over that amount, then search engines may penalize you the web page or site for keyword "spamming". Because of this, it's always preferable to know exactly what the search engines regard the perfect keyword density to be.

Keyword Prominence

is how close to the beginning of the area (META Tag content, body, etc...) that the keyword appears. In most cases, a keyword that appears or near the beginning of a META or HTML tag, near the top of the page, toward the start of a paragraph, will be more relevant.

Keyword Spamming

is the act of repeating keyword use on a web page way too much and thereby causing inflated keyword density. This improper practice is accomplished by stuffing keywords in HTML. Keyword spamming could result in a search engine penalizing the website for overuse and having an elevated keyword density. It's always best to maintain a keyword density of about 6 to 8%. Anything above that would be considered keyword spamming.

Keyword Stemming

is a process now implemented by Google and other search engines that search keywords as well as any variations of the keyword.

Keyword Tag, or META Keyword Tag

is an HMTL META Tag where multiple web page keywords are listed for the search engine spiders and robots to recognize. The Keyword Tag contents should not contain more than 10 or so keywords. The keywords that are listed should be the keywords that are found after conducting the Keyword Analysis procedure. Each separate web page can and should have completely different META Tag contents.

Keyword Targeting

is the practice of displaying Pay Per Click (PPC) advertisements unto Contextual Networks on the Internet. These ads specifically target keywords.

KPI (Key Performance Indicators)

are metrics employed to gauge the goals of a specific online marketing campaign. KPI provides knowledge about business and online marketing for the purpose of measuring progress and to determine the future course of that strategic objective.

L

Landing Page (Entry Page)

is a web page that a user is directed to when clicking on a link in a Search Engine Results Page (SERP) or Pay Per Click (PPC) advertisement.

Latent Semantic Indexing (LSI or Long Tail Searches)

is when word associations are used to assist search engines understanding about a particular web page. Most searches do contain a grouping of words (long tail), and the grouped words are much easier to optimize than single words like "Jewelry."

Lead Generation

is the process of generating leads for services or products located on a different website or physical location. On a lead generation website, a user is not permitted to purchase a product or service, but is rather given a form to fill out to request more information about how to do so. This form becomes the actual lead and usually contains personal information about a user who is interested in the product or service.

Link

is a text-string or graphical element on a web page that when clicked, will direct a user to a different web page, either within or without the current location of that link. Here is an HTML code example of a simple link:

```
<a    href="http://americreations.com>"    Maui
Web Design</a>
```

Search engines use links to "jump" from page to page while crawling the web.

Link Bait

is an element on a web page such as valuable content or high-quality services or products that other sites will take interest in and link to. When other sites link to you, they view the content as being of high quality and also believe that their site visitors will find it of interest as well. If many sites are linking to you, then that is an indication that you have interesting and valuable content.

Link Building

is the process of getting links to your site. There are several ways to perform this task. You could use online programs to acquire links, or the webmaster can contact other websites to request either a link exchange or that they provide a one-way link to your site. When link building, it is always recommended that you get links to your site from topically related or relevant websites; and also exchange links in a topical community.

Link Building Tactics

1. Develop resource lists for specific topics
2. Create a list of authority and hub sites.
3. Ensure that your site's content is unique, well written and well organized so your chances of getting backlinks will improve
4. Make certain that your site has no spelling or grammatical errors
5. Begin a PPC Campaign
6. Write articles and get them syndicated. You can put a link on all the articles you get published and there is a link pointing to your site. This is a great method!!!
7. Write a press release and submit it to all or a majority of press release syndicators
8. Contact other sites to exchange articles.
9. Have interactive (Web 2.0) features on your site to make users feel important
10. Submit your site to Web Directories
11. Submit your site to Paid Directories. Always ensure that if you pay for a listing that the director is of high quality
12. Enquire that your friends tag your news content so the content may have a chance of getting on Social Media sites, which will increase the chances that others will see the information and link to it
13. Submit a link to local directories and community pages
14. Ask all your friends and business associates to put a link to your site
15. Develop new business relationships and ask that they include a link to your site.
16. Create an Affiliate Program
17. Post ads at Craigslist.org

18. Submit a story to Digg that has a link to your site
19. Post a link with your signature at forums and blogs. Make appropriate blog posts that are smartly written and include a link to your site.
20. Review related products on Amazon.com. This process could result in an inbound link
21. Start your own blog and make regular posts to draw the attention of others who may end up linking to you
22. Link to other blogs and they most likely will link back
23. Link your new blog at blog directories
24. Exchange links with topically related websites
25. Become a sponsor to a charity or organization and they should provide a link to your site
26. Offer useful, intriguing tools that people will be interested in and link to
27. Be persistent and send many emails requiring that sites link to yours

Link Condom

is a use of the rel attribute that permits a webmaster to specify that a link has no trust. A link with a link condom applied (e.g. <a href="http://www.projectparadox.com/" rel="nofollow"> Site Anchor Text </a>) doesn't award any algorithmic ranking profit to the target site. In reality, a link condom thwarts the transfer of trust. Link condoms are mainly useful for webmasters because they also avert any harmful impact of linking out to awful neighborhoods. Various websites are marked as spam by search engines for a variety of reasons and linking to them can invite a ranking penalty for the linking site. By applying a link condom where useful, webmasters can make certain that user-submitted links do not hurt trust and rankings.

Link Exchange

is the process of reciprocating links with other websites. Link exchanges re often assisted by directory websites who main purpose is to exchange links with other sites. These particular directory pages are usually of no or extremely minimal purpose and benefit to those who link with them. It is always a preferable practice to manually exchange links with high quality, topically related sites. That process in itself could greatly increase your sites Link Popularity and thereby increase keyword rankings.

Link Farm

is a collection of sites who all link to one another. Grouping with a Link Farm is an outdated attempt to increase link popularity. This practice is considered a Black Hat SEO technique and is despised by the search engines. The problem with Link Farms is that you become linked with all types of website and mostly sites that have no topical relevance to your own site.

Link Juice

is a term that signifies trust, high PageRank, and authority. A current SEO slang term which basically means that a site it's referring to is trusted by the search engines and is (supposedly) an authority on the specific topic.

Link Love

refers to an outbound link that has earned trust and will not be inhibited in any way.

Link Partner's

are two website who link to one another. Because they are reciprocating links, these particular links usually do not carry as much value with the search engines.

Link Popularity

is the measurement of value of a website that is calculated by quality and quantity of the websites linking to it. There are Internal and External aspects to Link Popularity. Internal Link Popularity is calculated by the quantity of pages or links in a website that link to a particular single URL. External Link Popularity is calculated by the quantity of incoming links from other websites that all link to a particular URL.

Link Spam, or Comment Spam

is undesirable links that point to a site without permission from places like blogs, forums, and so on.

Link Superiority (link cardinality)

is a website that has more incoming links than their competitors.

Long Tail

are keyword search queries that are more specific and longer and usually contain 3 to 5 words. Long Tail keywords are less general than specific keywords and are employed to target specific topics. Most searches conducted on search engines are long tail searches. Conversion rates are generally optimal because they generate targeted users and are not general phrases, so the click-through rates are of higher value.

M

META Feeds

are advertisement networks that acquire ads from other suppliers.

META Tags

are HTML tags located between the <head> tags. META tags can contain a series of functions designed to give search engine spiders and robots information about a specific web page. Here's an example of META tags than taken directly from the author's site:

<meta name="keywords" content="Maui Web Design,American Creations,Maui Web Design,Affordable Websites,Graphic Design,Search Engine Optimization,Website Hosting,AMERICAN CREATIONS">

<meta name="Title" content= "Maui Web Design American Creations of Maui">

76

```html
<meta name="description" content= "Maui Web
Design by American Creations of Maui is an
affordable way to get an innovative and effective
website solution">

<meta name="author" content="American Creations
of Maui">

<meta name="copyright" content="American
Creations of Maui - Maui Website Design">

<meta name="rating" content="General">

<meta name="revisit-after" content="2 days">

<meta name="robots" content="FOLLOW, INDEX">

<meta name="distribution" content="Global">

<meta http-equiv="Content-Language" content="en-
us">

<meta http-equiv="reply-to"
content="terry@americreations.com">

<meta http-equiv="pragma" content="cache">

<meta http-equiv="Content-Type" content="text/html;
charset=us-ascii">

<meta http-equiv="PICS-Label" content="(PICS-
1.1">
```

It is extremely important to have specific and
unique content within the META Tags of each
different web page within a site. The search

engines depend on their content to determine what a web page is about. The META Title Tag is visible on the very top-left of your Internet browser and is the title of a web page. The META Description Tag contains a detailed description of the web page. Each search engine prefers a specific amount of words or characters for each tag and the amount of keywords within those tags. Please see Chapter 4 for more information.

Metric

in relation to SEO, is the type of measurement implemented by Analytics Programs. Some examples of metrics to measure in SEO is keyword rankings, top conversion and traffic driving keywords, conversions, search engine traffic, and overall traffic.

MFA (Made for Advertisements)

are websites that are specifically designed to function as an advertisement medium. MFAs' sole purpose is to advertise products, services, websites, events, organizations, or anything else that can be advertised.

Mirror Site

is a website that has been duplicated and is completely identical to its parent site. In regards to SEO, mirror site's are not beneficial and can actually get the parent or both sites penalized for having duplicate content. Search engines love and rank website whose content is original and unique much higher than websites that have identical content. Even duplicating content within the same site can hurt rankings, so always make sure that each page has relevant, unique content to keep search engines happy.

Monetize

is the process of earning income from a website. Some examples to monetize a website would be to add Affiliate Networks, Google's AdSense Ads, or having a "Sponsor" or advertisers program where people or businesses would pay to have an ad on your site.

N

Natural Search Results

are search engine results that are "natural" because these type of results occur naturally or "organically" without being sponsored or paying a fee.

NoFollow

is an HTML code command within a web page that instructs the search engine spiders or robots NOT to follow either all links on a web page or a specific link. NoFollow attributes may be added to any link by using the following HTML code:

<a href="http://www.siteurl.com" rel="nofollow" >
Site Anchor Text</a>

The NoFollow tag merely says to a search engine

to ignore this link as it is not to a 'trusted' resource. The page at the other end of the NoFollow link will not profit in PageRank. For instance, if you own an online gift shop and you want to or are asked to have a link to a non-relevant site such as a home builder site or an automotive site, then you can add a NoFollow attribute to that link so you are not voting or sending trust to that site or sites. This becomes extremely beneficial because search engines prefer that sites link to other topically related sites. NoFollow attributes can be extremely beneficial if used intelligently.

NoIndex

is a similar to the NoFollow Tag, but the NoIndex attribute instructs search engines spiders or robots to NOT index the specific web page or link. The NoIndex code can be found in either a specific link or between the <head> tags.

Non-Reciprocal Links

is a website that links to another website, but the website who the link is pointed towards does not link back.

O

Optimization

is the process of optimizing an object or website. For example, search engine optimization (SEO) is the process of optimizing or improving a website to achieve high keyword rankings and increased traffic. "Optimizing" a website may also refer to the process of reducing the file size of images and graphics and validating HTML code so that a website will have faster download times. For more detailed information on Search Engine Optimization, read this book of course, but also see Search Engine Optimization (SEO) in this Glossary.

Organic Results

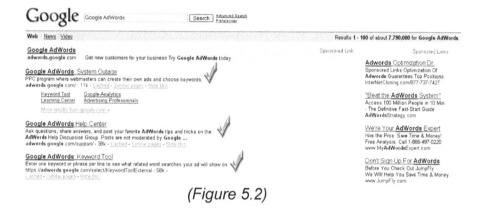

(Figure 5.2)

are SERP listings that appear naturally because the search engine believes that the site has quality or relevant content to the specific keyword query. Organic search results are not paid for or sold by search engines. They occur naturally through optimizing the site to achieve top rankings. Organic results are displayed under the Sponsored Listings, as illustrated in *figure 5.2*.

P

PageRank, (PR) or Google PageRank

is a value between 0 and 10 that calculates a sites importance by considering a site's link popularity, trust, and other determinants. PageRank was founded at Stanford University and its sole purpose is to place importance on websites and web pages. PageRank is one of the many factors that determine top search engine rankings.

Paid Inclusion (Guaranteed Inclusion)

is a way to guarantee inclusion in a search engine Index or Directory by paying a fee. Paid Inclusion are for people who don't feel like waiting 2 to 6 weeks for a search engine to Index a site or web page. When you pay the fee for Paid Inclusion, your site will be added to the search engine or directory much faster than if you don't pay. Usually there are different timeframes to choose from, and the charges would vary because of that. You may have to wait 24 to 48 hours, a week, or even a month in some cases. There are ways to speed up the process of getting a site or page indexed. For example, if you were able to get a backlink on a PR6 or above site, then your site will most likely get indexed within 1 to 3 days. Getting many backlinks will also speed up the process considerably.

Portal, or Web Portal

are sites such as Google, Yahoo, MSN, or AOL who provides a variety of features so a user will make their site their personal "Home Page". Portals usually contain a multitude of features like a search engine, weather, news, shopping, personals, and so on.

PPA (Pay Per Action)

is similar to PPC in that it's an advertising method, but with PPA publishers of ads only get paid when an action had been made from a click-through. A user would click on an ad link or banner and perform a specified action.

PPC (Pay Per Click)

is an advertising method similar to PPA, but with PPC a publisher would get paid for each click that it generates from the sites visitors. PPC ads are displayed on search engines, directories, AdWords, or websites and direct visitors to a specific landing page. The amount per click is usually determined by how strongly your desire is to rank higher than your competitors. PPC ads are based on bids and are influenced from your competitor's bids.

PPC Management

is the process of managing a PPC campaign or multiple campaigns. Similar to a webmaster managing a website, a PPC management technician would monitor and make the appropriate changes to a PPC campaign. If PPC Management is conducted properly and efficiently, then the conversion rates will escalate. A few examples of PPC Management include monitoring reports, analyzing keywords, making necessary adjustments to increase conversions, and so on.

Press Release

If you have a business and you have news, you need to announce it. Enter PR - public relations...or press releases...that other PR. As search engine marketing evolves towards traditional media marketing, this type of optimization will become more and more important. Understand the old methods of promotion, and it will help you to create effective strategies for new methods of promotion.

Press releases get you into a good habit of writing about and announcing news. These should be archived on your site as well. Use press releases to promote other forms of viral marketing that may be able to bring your site the links and recognition that you will need for higher rankings and growth. Pay for better distribution on the really important releases, and do free releases as practice for a bit of extra exposure. Check out all the places you can distribute (and I'm sure there are many more):

Q

Query

is a keyword or key phrase a search engine user enters in the search field so that the search engine will search and display the most trusted and relevant content associated with the particular keyword used.

R

Rank

is where a website or web page is listed in a SERP (Search Engine Results Page). Search engine rank is extremely important because search engines do generate most traffic to websites. Therefore, if a website or web page is ranked high in the search engines, then conversion rates and website/web page traffic increases. There can be an extraordinary difference in the amount of traffic to a web page between sites that ranks #1 or #2 than a site that ranks #11. SEO and internet marketing strives to get a site ranked high in the search engines.

Reciprocal Link

refers to two websites or pages that are linked together. Reciprocal links often result when a site owner or webmaster contacts another site to request a link exchange. It may also occur through software that automatically exchanges links with sites.

Redirect

is when a site or page is sent to a different location and can happen several different ways. There are 301 and 302 Redirects and domain redirects

Relevance

in relation to PPC advertising, is a measurement of the relevance, or closeness, an ad is to the user's search keyword. Relevance measures a variety of aspects, including ad title, ad description, and the keywords used in the ad. The ad will rank higher if its relevance factor is the closest to the search keyword used. Search engines use an algorithm to determine relevance when users enter a keyword or key phrase.

Regional Long Tail (RLT)

is a keyword consisting of 2 or more words that contains a city or region name. Regional long tail keyword phrases are often used with sites that offer a service. If you own a site that repairs automobiles, then using a RLT such as Maui Automotive Repair, or Maui Oil Change would be a good example.

Robots.txt

is a file read specifically by search engine robots and spiders and are used to manage where search engines crawl your site. If you do not want a spider or robot to search a specific web page or pages, then you would instruct them not to in the robots.txt file located in the root directory of your website. The robots.txt file is also used to direct the crawlers where to crawl. Here is an example of a proper robots.txt file:

```
User-agent: *
Disallow: /guestbook
Disallow: /images
```

```
Disallow: /image
Disallow: /post.php
Disallow: /post.pl
Disallow: /post.cgi
Disallow: /search.php
Disallow: /search.cgi
User-agent: stress-agent
Disallow: /
```

ROI (Return on Investment)

is the amount of income you earn on your ads or marketing campaign compared to the amount of money you spend on the ads or campaign. For example, if you spend $1000.00 on PPC ads and make $1500.00 form these ads, then your ROI on that campaign would be 50%. It should be your goal as a site owner or webmaster/SEO/Internet marketer to get a high ROI on all campaigns by efficient and intelligent ad management.

RSS (Really Simply Syndication or Rich Site Summary)

is a web feed program used to distribute regularly updated page content like blogs, news sites, podcasts, and video. RSS feeds syndicate, or share and distribute, information to all those who subscribe to the feed.

S

Saturation

in relation to SEO, is the quantity of web pages indexed in a search engine for a particular website.

Saturation is also referred to as Search Engine Saturation. It is generally accepted and proven that a higher saturation level will produce higher potential traffic and higher rankings.

Search Engine (SE)

is a database of a large quantity of web pages where users go to enter specific search keywords to locate relevant websites to acquire information and knowledge. Search engines use complex algorithms to rank web pages for a given keyword/ key phrase. Search engine algorithms are different, so rankings usually vary between the different search engines.

SEM (Search Engine Marketing)

is the process of marketing that is done to draw more traffic to websites by increasing search engine rankings. SEM is usually different than Search Engine Optimization (SEO) because it also involves PPC management, SEO, paid listings, and so on. SEMs ultimate goal is to attract more visitors to a website.

SEO (Search Engine Optimization)

is the process of drawing more visitors to a website by optimizing keywords to get high search engine rankings. Because search engines generate most traffic to websites, conducting SEO on a website is extremely crucial and may be the determining factor of whether a website will succeed or fail. Properly conducted SEO techniques and practices will usually always draw more traffic to a website. SEO includes many things. Here's a basic summary of the tasks involved in SEO:

1. Keyword Factors:
   * Keyword Research.
   * Optimize keyword use within the title tag, body text, H1 tag, domain name, H2 and H3 tags, alt tags, bold/strong tags, META description tag, META keywords tag, and focus on the keyword density.
2. On-Page Factors:
   * Validate HTML code to comply with W3C Standards.
   * Validate CSS code to comply with W3C Standards.
   * Organizational layout
   * Link popularity
   * Relevance of links to external sites
   * Quality of content
   * Update pages frequently
   * Spelling and grammar corrections
3. Inbound Link Factors:
   * Anchor text of inbound link
   * Global link popularity of linking Site
   * Topical relationship of linking Page
   * Google PageRank of linking page
4. Website accessibility
5. Get indexed quickly by search engine spiders and crawlers like Googlebot
6. Directory and Niche directory submissions
7. Search Engine Ranking Reports
8. Submit your site to search engines on a regular basis.
9. Website Competitive Intelligence
10. Google Sitemap Creation & Submission

11.   Robots.txt optimization
12.   Proper use of NoIndex and NoFollow Tags
13.   Externalizing scripts
14.   Integration/optimization of themed pages (if necessary)
15.   Ongoing Optimization Updates

SERP (Search Engine Results Page)

is the page that a search engine reveals after a keyword/key phrase has been entered and submitted. SERPs display both sponsored and organic or "natural" listings. SERPs display web pages by order of importance, as each particular search engine believes to be, starting with the most important or relevant web page.

Sitemap

is a web page or collection of organized pages that link to every user-accessible web page on a site. Sitemaps are also useful to visitors who may have issues navigating through a website. Another form of sitemap is an XML Sitemap that is used by search engines to locate and crawl each page of a website. Here is an example of a real, live Google XML Sitemap:

```
<?xml version="1.0" encoding="UTF-8"?>
<urlset
xmlns="http://www.sitemaps.org/schemas/sitemap/0.9"
     xmlns:xsi="http://www.w3.org/2001/XMLSchema-
instance"

xsi:schemaLocation="http://www.sitemaps.org/schema
s/sitemap/0.9
```

```
http://www.sitemaps.org/schemas/sitemap/0.9/sitemap.
xsd">
<url>
 <loc>http://americreations.com/</loc>
 <priority>1</priority>
 <lastmod>2008-03-22T19:42:40+00:00</lastmod>
 <changefreq>weekly</changefreq>
</url>
<url>
 <loc>http://americreations.com/mauiwebdesign.html
</loc>
 <priority>1</priority>
 <lastmod>2008-03-22T19:42:40+00:00</lastmod>
 <changefreq>weekly</changefreq>
</url>
<url>

<loc>http://americreations.com/graphicdesign.html</loc
>
 <priority>1</priority>
 <lastmod>2008-03-22T19:42:40+00:00</lastmod>
 <changefreq>weekly</changefreq>
</url>
<url>
 <loc>http://americreations.com/webhosting.html</loc>
 <priority>1</priority>
 <lastmod>2008-03-22T19:42:40+00:00</lastmod>
 <changefreq>weekly</changefreq>
</url>
<url>
 <loc>http://americreations.com/bookpublishing.html
</loc>
 <priority>1</priority>
 <lastmod>2008-03-22T19:42:40+00:00</lastmod>
 <changefreq>weekly</changefreq>
</url>
```

```
<url>
 <loc>http://americreations.com/marketing.html</loc>
 <priority>1</priority>
 <lastmod>2008-03-22T19:42:40+00:00</lastmod>
 <changefreq>weekly</changefreq>
</url>
<url>
 <loc>http://americreations.com/contact.html</loc>
 <priority>1</priority>
 <lastmod>2008-03-22T19:42:40+00:00</lastmod>
 <changefreq>weekly</changefreq>
</url>
<url>
 <loc>http://americreations.com/links.html</loc>
 <priority>1</priority>
 <lastmod>2008-03-22T19:42:40+00:00</lastmod>
 <changefreq>weekly</changefreq>
</url>
<url>
 <loc>http://americreations.com/freequote.html</loc>
 <priority>1</priority>
 <lastmod>2008-03-22T19:42:40+00:00</lastmod>
 <changefreq>weekly</changefreq>
</url>
<url>
 <loc>http://americreations.com/graphicdesignportfolio.
html</loc>
 <priority>1</priority>
 <lastmod>2008-03-22T19:42:40+00:00</lastmod>
 <changefreq>weekly</changefreq>
</url>
</urlset>
```

Sitemap's are "maps" for users and search engines. Google has implemented a free sitemap service where webmasters can submit website SML

Sitemaps to Google. Google will then crawl the Sitemap and Index, more than likely, all the pages listed in it.

Social Bookmark

is a technique for Internet users to accumulate, manage, explore, and administer bookmarks of web pages on the Internet with the assistance of metadata. In a social bookmarking structure, users save links to web pages that they wish to access and/or share. These bookmarks are typically public, and can be saved confidentially, shared only with particular people or groups, shared only within certain networks, or another combination of public and private domains. The permitted people can generally view these bookmarks chronologically, by category or tags, or by means of a search engine. Here's a list of Social Bookmarking Services:

BlinkBits	My-Tuts
BlinkList	Netscape
Blogmarks	Netvouz
Buddymarks	Newsvine
CiteUlike	NShout
del.icio.us	Onlywire
Diigo	PlugIM
DZone	RawSugar
Earthlink	RecommendzIt
FeedMarker	reddit
Flog this!	Scuttle!
Feedmelinks	SearchMob
Furl	Segnalo
Google	Shadows
Give a Link	Simpy
Gravee	Sphinn
igooi	Spurl

ISEdb Scoop   Squidoo
Lilisto   StumbleUpon
Linkagogo   Taggly
Linkroll   tagtooga
Looklater   TalkDigger
ma.gnolia   Tellfriends
Maple.nu   Wink
Marktd   Yahoo MyWeb
Mr. Wong

Social Media

is a wide array of online technologies that people use to share and distribute information.

Basic forms of social media:

Social networks
Wikis
Podcasts
Content communities
Microblogging

Most Popular Social Media Sites:

1. Digg	16. Flickr
2. Del.icio.us	17. WikiHow
3. Reddit	18. BlueDot
4. Technorati	19. StyleHive
5. Squidoo	20. JotSpot
6. Netscape	21. Wetpaint
7. LinkedIn	22. Shadows
8. Newsvine	23. Yahoo! 360
9. Wikipedia	24. Furl

10. Ma.gnolia	25. Ning
11. StumbleUpon	26. Frappr
12. Shoutwire	27. The Best Stuff In The World
13. Facebook	28. MySpace
14. 43 Things	29. Yahoo! Answers
15. YourElevatorPitch	30. Rdiculous

Spamming

refers to technologies that do not adhere to search engine guidelines and are scams that deceptively trick the search engines. Spamming includes Black Hat SEO tactics like hidden text, content replication, doorway pages, Link Farms, etc....

Spider (Robot or Crawler)

is a program that is designed to assist search engines in gathering data from websites by crawling link structures and using an algorithm to rank web pages. Spiders index their findings into the search engines so that keyword queries will access the data.

Splash Page

is usually an opening page on a website that contains, usually, animated graphics such as Flash effects to "attract" the attention of visitors by appeal to the eye. Splash pages do not necessarily have to be animated, but they usually are. Search engines have difficulty crawling Splash pages because most of them are animated and search engine crawlers can only search text. Search engines are finally becoming able to search Flash objects; however, in relation to SEO, Splash pages should always be avoided to maximize chances of receiving high rankings. There are other, more efficient and logical approaches to draw the attention of visitors. Using a Flash header with effects is a perfect alternative.

Sponsored Listing

refers to the term that SERPs used to feature and list paid advertisers and to separate paid advertisement and organic (natural) listings.

Static Page

is a non-dynamic web page. Static pages are used to better conform to search engine guidelines because static pages have a permanent location without session IDs in the Url. Because of this, static pages are friendly to search engine crawlers.

Submission

is the process of submitting a website to a search engine or directory.

T

TLP (Top Level Page)

are web pages that are in the top levels of a site's directory. TLPs usually refer to the Home Page, About Page, Product or Services Page, Contact

Page, and any other "important" web page that have specific importance to the site.

Tail Terms

are search terms which are extremely specific in nature. Tail terms are long phrases.

Targeting

is the process of focusing ads to reach a specific audience. Targeting is essential to achieve top performance from ad campaigns and SEO. First, a site owner or webmaster would determine, possibly after thorough research, who, exactly, is most likely going to purchase the service or product. You can "target" ads on a specific search engine, geographic location, niche directories, times, behavioral targeting, and so on.

Text Link

is an html link that contains a text string without the use of graphics or dynamic content. The text of the link is called the Anchor Text, and is essential in SEO and achieving top rankings.

Title Tag

is an HTML Tag that is located between the <head> tags and is used to display the page title in the Internet browser. The Title Tag is also very important to SEO and should be optimized with the correct amount of keywords and total words used, including Keyword Prominence.

Toolbar PageRank (PR)

is the same thing as PageRank, which is a value between 0 and 10 that calculates a sites importance by considering a sites link popularity, trust, and other determinates. For more information, please see PageRank.

Topical Relevance

Topically relevant websites are sites that have similar or related content. The search engines, especially Google, are including these "relevance" factors in their search algorithms. Because of this, all site owners should thoroughly search for and request link exchanges with topically relevant sites.

Tracking URL

is a precisely built and unique URL that has been developed to track actions/conversions from paid ads. Tracking URLs often contain strings that reveal the keywords used, search engines who sent the user, and so on.

Traffic

is the quantity of visitors to a website. There are sophisticated statistics program such as AwStats, Urchin Statistics, and Google Analytics to name a few that reveal site statistics including traffic. Traffic used to be measured by "Hits," but that is an outdated method because hits are counted every time a page opens, and for every image or object on each page when the page opens. A more accurate method in accurately determining how many true visitors a site receives is to count the Page Views.

Traffic Analysis

is the procedure of analyzing website traffic to determine exactly what is drawing visitors to a site. Traffic Analysis would include analyzing the exact keywords that are bringing the site visitors, what search engines are referring visitors, what backlinks visitors are clicking on to get to the site, how many hits the site is getting, how long visitors are staying on each web page, and also what pages visitors are most often leaving the site. After discovering these factors, SEO specialists can take the required steps to increase hits and all other aspects to bring more site visitors.

Trusted Feed

or Paid Inclusion, is a service offered by search engines to crawl sites by requiring a fee. The results are listed in the organic results. Trusted feeds are a way to submit information to search engines, instead of search engines actually crawling the site.

U

Unique Visitor

is a way of measuring exactly how many unique users are searching a website. If one user views several different web pages on a website, that user is still considered one unique visitor.

Usability (User-Friendly or Accessibility)

is how user friendly a site is. Many factors determine the usability, such as data organization, navigational structure, font styles, use of images, dynamic functions, html code, and so on.

When checking for site usability, you should review the following areas:

    Design Process and Evaluation
    Accessibility
    Hardware and Software
    The Homepage
    Page Layout
    Navigation
    Scrolling and Paging
    Headings, Titles, and Labels
    Links
    Text Appearance
    Lists
    Screen–Based Controls
    Graphics, Images, and Multimedia
    Writing Web Content
    Content Organization
    Search

URL (Uniform Resource Locator)

also referred to as a Web Address. A URL is a specific web page and begins with a specific domain name. For example,

...is a URL.

V

Vertical Market Search Engine

is a topical search engine that typically targets a specific topic of interest. A niche website that contains a search engine is an example.

W

W3C (The World Wide Web Consortium)

According to the W3C website, "W3C primarily pursues its mission through the creation of Web standards and guidelines. Since 1994, W3C has published more than 110 such standards, called W3C Recommendations. W3C also engages in education and outreach, develops software, and serves as an open forum for discussion about the Web. In order for the Web to reach its full potential, the most fundamental Web technologies must be compatible with one another and allow any hardware and software used to access the Web to work together."

Web 2.0

refers to websites that encourage user interaction. Here is a list of features that comprise Web 2.0:

- User generated and/or user influenced content
- Applications that use the Web (versus the desktop) as a platform, in innovative ways
- Similar visual design and shared functional languages
- Leveraging of popular trends, including blogging, social tagging, wikis, and peer-to-peer sharing
- Inclusion of emerging web technologies like RSS, AJAX, APIs (and accompanying mashups), Ruby on Rails and others
- Open source or sharable/editable frameworks in the form of user-oriented "create your own" APIs
- Multimedia sharing

According to Tim O'Reilly's article titled, "What is Web 2.0," he explains the difference between Web 1.0 and Web 2.0 in this table:

Web 1.0   Web 2.0

Web 1.0	Web 2.0
DoubleClick	Google AdSense
Ofoto	Flickr
Akamai	BitTorrent
mp3.com	Napster
Britannica Online	Wikipedia
personal websites	blogging
evite	upcoming.org and EVDB
domain name speculation	search engine optimization
page views	cost per click
screen scraping	web services
publishing	participation
content management systems	wikis
directories (taxonomy)	tagging ("folksonomy")
stickiness	syndication

Web Forwarding

permits redirects to inhabit within an .htaccess file on a different server.

White Hat

are SEO strategies and techniques that adhere to best practice guidelines set by the search engines. White Hat SEO is "ethical" SEO practices without deception or using underground techniques. Here's a list of some White Hat SEO tactics:

- Preparing Genuine Content
- Proper Title Formatting
- Meta Tags (with Relevant page related keywords)
- Proper usage of Header Tags

- Internal linking pattern (with relevant page linking)
- Not using any Hidden Text or Links (Hiding with by CSS or by HTML Code)
- Not participating in any Affiliated Link Exchange or Link Farms.
- No Link Trading with bad Neighborhood sites. (site banned by search engines)
- Not spamming any blogs, forums, guest books (for getting any back links)
- Proper usage of robots.txt file (guiding search engines which files or directory to index) or not)

Widget, see Gizmo for more information.

Wiki

is software that enables users to contribute and submit information on certain topics.

X

XML (Extensible Markup Language)

is a markup language that is used to deliver data.

XML Feeds

are a method of paid inclusion where search engines are fed data about an advertiser's web pages by way of XML, instead of the search engine having to crawl the web pages manually. XML feeds are fee-based and usually charge by the URL or CPC basis. XML feeds assure site owners that the search engines will frequently crawl their web pages.

XML Sitemap

is a sitemap or list of links to the pages on a website in XML. XML Maps are used by the search engines to locate all the pages of a website. For an example of an XML Sitemap, please see Sitemap.

INDEX

Y

Yahoo · vii, 11, 13, 35, 46, 62, 67, 82, 93, 94, 95

Yahoo Announcement Groups · 13

Notes

About the Author

Terry Dunford, owner of American Creations of Maui, is a web design and search engine optimization professional and also is an expert in graphic design, business marketing, internet marketing, technical writing, book editing, photography, videography, book editing and publishing. Terry has 4 years of college training in web development and marketing; Terry also has training in writing and business.

Terry Dunford was born and raised in Bakersfield, California, and now resides in Maui, Hawaii, where he enjoys a wonderful life with his lovely wife, Debra and three dogs: Baby Maxwell, Britney aka "Extra Big Buddy," and Little cutie aka "Little Stinker."

Terry and his business American Creations of Maui has become one of Maui and Hawaii's leading and most recognized web design and search engine optimization company. Terry now has more than 60 regular extremely happy and long-standing clients.

Terry's hobbies include writing, gardening, spear fishing, and ballroom dancing with his beautiful wife, Debra. Terry has spent years researching search engine optimization practices and techniques, while also putting his knowledge to good use by getting all of his clients top rankings in the search engines.

American Creations of Maui
45 Uahaa Pl., Wailuku, HI 96793
terrydunford@yahoo.com
www.americreations.com
(808) 250-2524

Price: $16.95

www.ingramcontent.com/pod-product-compliance
Lightning Source LLC
Chambersburg PA
CBHW051245050326
40689CB00007B/1076